Devine Timing

Jennifer Jewell

BookLeaf
Publishing

Presentation by *BookLeaf Publishing*

Web: www.bookleafpub.com

E-mail: info@bookleafpub.com

ISBN: 9789357212281

First edition 2023

DEDICATION

I dedicate these poems to ALL of the
individuals that have struggled, and continue to
struggle with Addiction.

I also dedicate this to the many that did not
survive, and to the many families that have lost
a loved one to these demon's of death.

Further more, I dedicate my admiration to the
Angels that have been brought to light my way
through the darkness! There are so many...I am
entirely blessed to be alive and to share this
journey with you all! I am living proof that
through faith and our higher powers, it is
possible.

Special dedication to Turning Point detox
center in Grand Rapids Michigan, also to Henry
Ford Alliance Rehabilitation Center in Jackson
Michigan.

Most of all, to my two beautiful daughters,
Taylor and Trinity. There are not enough words
to explain how much strength and love you
both have given back to me when I needed it

the most. All my family and friends, I wouldn't be who I am without your constant encouragement.

Michael K, you have been my forever mentor that changed my life.

Dawn H, Lonny C, Kelly S, Shannon D James S, Amanda P, Roger A,Linda M, Josh M, Joshua D, Charles (CR) , Dorian Paul. Lynette, Adam, Chris S, Patricia L, Victor D, Korina, Daryl D, Carly B, Shirley E, Linda R, Patricia S(adopted Big Sis) My boss Alan S, Dr Jeanine Ernest and most of all To Dale and BettyLue Jewell (My loving Parents who watch and have kept me safe from above)

Also to the haters, gossipers, and manipulators that helped me remember each day why I stay sober!!

You all are my forever Angels!

ACKNOWLEDGEMENT

"You cannot get to heaven, if you haven't felt the heat of hell"
JJJEWELL
My Acknowledgement goes to every person that woke us this morning and chose life!
To the countless Addicts that are living in strife.
From the North and to the South, and the East and West, continuously fighting when life is put to the test!
To the hundreds and thousands that are dying inside, our higher power gives us strength when heaven and hell collide.
You were born to be a fighter, humbling and true, there's never a day that I have not thought of you.
Stand firm and solid as each day passes, watch your life get better as we take these impeccable chances.
The gift of life is around the corner you will cry these tears no longer!!
JJJEWELL 🖤

PREFACE

"Dying was the easy part, coming back from death is truly when life became real"
JJJEWELL 🖤

"ADDICTION is the REALEST of the REAL"
JJJEWELL 🖤

Inspiration

It's not very often that I'm speechless and amazed, life keeps getting better now that I'm not running in a maze.

Twisting and turning running into walls, panicking and frantic duty now calls

It is calling me, by my full name requiring my mind to be present this is not a game

I haven't felt a purpose as much as I do now, waking up to a sunrise being reminded that someone knew somehow

You took the time to capture a moment, that you shared only with me..that brought you happiness my forever friend Kelly.. You forever inspire me!!

I am looking so forward to being able to give that back..friends like you are far between, for sure keeps us on track

I see the beautiful sunlight that I never want to go away...Thank God made us friends to encourage us both, every step of the way...

My Good Friend Kelly S.. We sure are blessed!!
Much Love Always...with a hint of Vanilla and
Spunk!!

12-2-22 JJJEWELL 🖤

Triggered

Silent but deadly as you creep inside my soul,
aching and hardly breathing wanting to smoke
that glass bowl

Inhaling that demon that I wrestle every day, I'm
here at rehab praying why can't you go the hell
away?

Fragile and guilty that I chose you over my life,
erasing all my good memories leaving me
wounded completely in strife

Clawing and screaming for you to go away, as
the crystals fill my lungs come on week one,
come out and play

I cling on to your sins and whisper to you while
you sleep, tell you to keep shooting up... There
is no room for you to foolishly weep!!

I creep through the goodness and purity you
once had, cardiac arrest I long for when you cry
and you are sad

What? Why are you fighting me you stupid cursed soul, now you're pulling away from me not allowing me to rock and roll

Somehow you are defeating me with your buddies at AA, shutting me down so I can no longer stay

I am a part of you, whenever you call, laughing hysterically at you while you pray and bawl

This man you call God has filled your once desperate Heart, you finally chose you you think you are so smart

Thank you Lord for saving me, and loving me still, you never have forsaken me only instilled this incredible will

The will to dry my tears and forgive me again, for this I will remain alive for you did not condemn

I'm speechless and free to begin this precious life, my heart beats again for now I hold the knife

The knife resembles power which you no longer bestow I took it all back now just look at my radiant glow

7-1-22 JJJEWELL ♥

The Road

When the road is hard, and you feel that you
have failed, and the breath you breathe is
frantically inhaled,
Just close your eyes and take that step, for God
will hold you, carry and protect.

In memory of the late Dale John Jewell
10-21-41 to 08-27-2000
My Daddy JJJEWELL ♥

Echo

Did you hear that sound?
that echo's from within?
The beating of the heart
clean and healthy from sin

Finally taking time
to listen to ones self
Whispering I Love You
praising your healing bill of health

Waking up today
was different than the rest
Calm, cool, and collective
as my hand is placed on my chest

I opened up my eyes
realizing it's not a dream
Smiling and Thankful
as peaceful water running in a stream

I chose sobriety today
while counting 61 days
Clear mined and inspired
feels too good to let go away

7-9-22 JJJEWELL 🖤

Z Money

Making an impact
is not an easy gift
Inspiring ones self
You must first uplift

Gratitude and Patience
fills you're weakend mind
Breaking you down gently
Vulnerable and sacrifice made you kind

I knew you had a gift
the first moment we met
Allowing your true self to shine
as we all read, prayed and wept

You dried away out tears
with your compassionate ways
Leading us all profoundly
never forgetting to give us praise

You are a precious leader
so much you have over come
Standing tall while cooking bacon
sharing it with some

God has prepared you
for this next bold step
He will never mis-lead you
For he will hold you and protect

Get out there Brave Murphy
and give it you're all
Your forever family here knows
you might trip, but never fall

Here comes the Real Talk
as our eyes are filled with tears
You are FOREVER our brother
completely blessed for our upcoming sober and
clean years

It is now your time
to shine bright as a star
We wish you forever happiness
call out if you need us, we are never far

JJJEWELL ♥ 7-12-22
 Z Money was my first friend, leader, and
Inspiration to me when I was in Henry Ford
Allience Rehabilitation Jackson Mi..Thank You
Zach

Flat-Lined

I hate the feeling
of being Up and Down
Twirling about
On a merry-go-round

Being pushed to the side
all day long
Nobody can approach me
my aura seems to strong

It's a feeling I feel
that I cannot control
It's burning so bad
and irritating my soul

Raw elbows and knees
as I constantly bleed
Blurring every word
that I am trying to read

My eyes are filled
with nothing but tears,
When will this feeling leave
seems like it has stuck for years

Violently racing
as it's causing me such pain,
I truly wish it could be washed away
Washed away like the rain

I'm screaming inside
for someone to help
NOBODY'S COMING
I feel like running

Running away?
Or towards the drug?
It's something I cannot control
Nor push under the rug

I'm silently dying
Screaming so loud
Here comes the wind
the hovering big black cloud

It's either here to save me
Or to take my life
Over coming my spirit
Leaving me in violent strife

Pushing and Pulling
 to get me to give in
Does anybody feel
What I'm feeling within

I'm lost and alone
boy, imagine that
I'm shaking and crying
Please yell CODE...then flat

Flat is the baseline
where I no longer feel
Is this the end?
Are you seriously for real?

Where is the glory
that everyone sees?
Where is the bright light
as I'm praying on my knees

I hate what you have done
to your angry destructive self,
Dont look for pity
within yourself!!
8-20-22 JJJEWELL ♥

The Sacrifice

Rebirth doesn't come by chance, nor did my
addiction of death.
 ..Sentenced by my addicted soul clouded by the
rolling smoke of meth

Clinging to this new found high that captured
my mind and soul, Floating onward into the
dark goodbye.. I'm on one hell of a roll

Cheating, lying, begging and stealing the
precious moments of time. Laughing torture fun
and games the death was going to be mine

Sacrificing the love of a child not just one, but
two. My beautiful elegant daughters soon will be
saying my mom who?

Who is that woman that talks of Love while
selling herself so short. We cannot stand this
selfish witch let her smoke, lie, and snort

Our mother no longer exists furthermore, we
really don't care. She picked her newfound
friendly life regret, hate and loneliness is all hers
to bare.

You no longer have a daughter not one, nope
that makes two. No family, friends, or parents...
You smart girl, look at you!!

Pathetic and embarrassing we cannot tell a lie,
you chose your awesome new people now you
can rot because soon you will die!

Finally, the clouds parted then Jennifer really
then knew. If she did not surrender now, she
would never see the sky again blue

Some days after a restful sleep completely
owning what she had done. While molding and
while healing another Life For Me has just
begun

I was able to wake at 5:00 a.m. all by my sober
self. I saw the amazing horizon maybe for the
first time all in itself

Choosing sobriety has been easy it's staying
sober is the hard part. Letting go of self-doubt
and demons has helped me know I still have a
heart

My cup is empty and I need refilled for all my
goodness I stupidly gave away. My children are
what I need, I am praying for that day

The day where their arms are open and
forgiveness is on their face. I keep praying to my
Lord please tell me I gave them enough space

Taylor and Trinity my two blessings from above
I will never again forsake forgive me all I have
left is love

You both are not children you are now the
strongest women, you have put me in my place
and stood tall with meaningful Grace

I brought you both up to stand on your own two
feet fight against All odds even your mother you
must defeat

Not because you hate her or wish her
permanently dead only because you have loved
her and cannot wait to kiss her on her forehead

This is all that I am and this is all I will be I
forgiven myself finally I can now be set free

Contemplation

Ignorance is a bliss ...so they say, Are you just
ignoring the fact or plain running away?

Burying your head in that deep cold sand,
instead of asking for help or a strong steady
hand

Owning your shortcomings and admitting your
pain leaves you no room to continue living life
in shame

I hear you crying, crying so desperately loud,
taking your own life Jennifer, will only ensure
You Hell bound

Do you want to live, or do you want to die? Rise
above ridicule, or is it eye for an eye?

Significantly hoping you choose yourself, you
may be broke, but living clean gives you more
wealth

You don't get to give up, and cheat this life you
have left, it's full of oppurtuity, it's been heaven
sent

Put down the needle, and the glass pipe... It's time you stood tall, now get up and fight!

The Moment

When it comes to knowing you,(lol) You better figure it out, ooo girl, better get a clue, so reason to scream and shout

It's time to stand don't be sitting down, walk softly but quickly gracefully, without a sound

You are here for a reason no doubt in my mind, changing the world, embracing mankind

Proudly to be the victim of no more hurt or shame, no more overthinking, those clouds only bring rain

Take a deep breath, No looking Back no questioning the reason, fate has you write on track

Becoming one with the moment requires you to slow down, hold hands a little longer, give that radiant smile never a frown

Did you see what just happened, a new life has begun !! You are now 5 months sober, that you have successfully done

I see with brand new eyes and here with new
ears, patients, discipline, and Recovery will
forever be no more wasted years

You have come to the finish line where your life
has now turned, you are about to be blessed
every miracle you now have earned.

10-3-22

My Savior

They say that misery loves company, depending on what kind of company you Keep... Do they use you for a side hustle, make your bed all nice and neat?

Do they pray for you in your time of need, or do they laugh hysterically while you bleed

Would they pick you up when you're walking, or are they afraid if people begin talking

Kindness and understanding is free it doesn't cost you a thing how do I know this? This person is me

I've walked to the dark through the violent wind and rain, I've crossed miles and valleys held my head entirely in shame

One day I met a man that reminded me I was more precious than gold, give me words and the strength to remind people that our story goes never untold

He wiped my eyes and held me close, taught me
to stand when I was weakened the most

Reminded me that there is forgiveness and a
beautiful life ahead, I was meant to share people
sorrow, yesterday, today's , and all of tomorrows

Chances

From the north and to the south, and the East
and the West, continuously fighting when life
puts us to the test

To the hundreds and thousands that are dying
inside, our higher power gives us strength when
heaven and Hell collide

You were born to be a fighter humbling and true,
there's never a day that I have not thought of you

Stand firm and solid as each day passes, your
life gets better as we take these impeccable
chances
12-1-22 JJJEWELL ♥

Man of my Dreams

Nothing seems meaningless while you are
running through my mind, hardworking and
devoted compassionate in oh so kind

Gently you try to explain when I don't
understand, tears roll down my cheeks as you
wipe them gently, like a real man

I have been waiting for a long long time, you
came to me in such a shock, putting your hand
in mine

Your lips look so inviting as you hold me in your
arms, your warmth is so amazing, you smile at
me with so much charm

Is this just a dream should I attempt to open my
eyes ? zYou truly have come to grow, lovee, and
compromise

I decided this very day, to thank God from
above, would he finally make a way and finally
bless me Dorian, with your forever love

12-7-22 JJJEWELL ♥

Keep It Moving

When do we become a Man or Woman?

I don't believe it is at 18, 21 or when we bore our first child.

It's when we lose our mother or father. They don't tell us this for fear of terrifying us and US losing sight of our potential, and it's extremely short lifetime

We then are handed the torch, for now becomes our strength that we
acquired through their death. It is now a reminder that we must keep the fire burning, and we must move forward.

To the money that have lost their mother or father, they are still here, paving the way to your success, they never left as long as you keep it moving.

12/2/22 JJJEWELL ♥

Do You Know?

Do you know what it's like to be vulnerable and
in pain, do you know what it's like for people to
leave you in shame?

Do you know how hard it is to start over from
the beginning, do you know how hard it is when
it feels like the devil is winning?

Do you know how hard it is to leave your past
behind, automatically supposed to acclimate
recover, restart, and rewind?

Have you ever felt peace in the short lifetime,
have you ever felt forgiveness and just wanted it
to be mine?

Did you ever see that shadow that follows you
on the ground, did you ever see that shadow
touching you all around?

Was it an angel or a demon that kept you away,
was it an angel or demon that was begging you
to stay?

Did you ever feel that moment when you chose yourself, did you ever feel that moment when you embrace your health?

Do you know what it's like to give your heart away, to a world and its rules that make you go insane?

Do you know what it's like to pick your ass up off the ground, one legacy and loneliness is spending you round and round?

It's time to get off the merry-go-round, that spins you a hundred times and throws you to the ground

Choose wisely every chance you get, no more room for guilt no more room for regret

But the spirit Now set you free, why you say? Because I know just chose me

How did that feel when you can be real, did it excite or leave you in fright?

You completely deserve everything in time, my precious person you now bring the sunshine

Open up the curtains and see this beautiful life,
that is not meant to hurt you but it wiser through
hurtful strife

Do you know how it feels to have no more
bogus drug deals?

You are meant to be
everything you are
Embrace it, and grab
Your beautiful star

Awakening

Fire in my eyes while chasing this high, blood's pumping quickly I'm peacefully looking at the sky

My breath is now shallow and my eyes are heavy, I just want to close them I'm calm, still, and ready

The silence is now fading The echoes no longer loud, I feel sky high like I'm floating on a cloud

This is not my death where I exit from this earth, for this was my spiritual Awakening my humble, gratifying, rebirth

8-12-22 JJJEWELL 🖤

Dorian's Inspiration

Are you asleep or are you awake? Your first
night at detox, are you thinking you made a
mistake?

Are you feeling the withdrawal, like poison in
your veins, desperately aching, your body feels
when it rains

Is it cloudy and loud, or do you prefer no more
sound?

Is your heart beating hard, harder than it should?
Are you grabbing at your chest, like a heart
attack would?

No wait, we haven't even got to the best part!
The mind fricken trickery, where should we
start?

It's not so funny when we are in agony and in
pain, that demon stole all dignity, left you losing
the game

Hold up, dont be afraid, Hurry up and slam some
Jose. Spinning you round and round, and around
again...cry, gag and curse this unbearable sin.

Awe, why are you crying? Did you overdo it?
Lost your family, and children while Yelling
Screw It?

I don't feel sorry for you, not one damn bit, is
this finally enough, to make you quit?

Now who is screwed, without a clue, or what to
do, to finally fix you?

I will leave you with this thought, that A very
wise man taught
If you talk the talk, you must walk the walk. Eat
crow like a man, do the best you can. Detox is
your start, my hero dorian, you now play the
part.
Rehab will hold your hand, if you are brave
enough to stand. The sun will now shine, for you
are right on time. It's time to live, not die,
finding these answers up in the sky.. Why? You
are about to see miracles that money can never
buy

10-26-22 JJJEWELL ♥

Seven

Simplicity at its best the devil putting us to the test, will you fail, or will you win, if you choose right, again life will begin it won't come very easily right from the start, to be exceptionally honest it will tear your life apart

Accepting we fall victim to all the seven deadly sins, don't give up my darling you'll allow the demons to win
PRIDE- It will take you for one hell of a ride
GREED- Forever selfishly you will bleed
LUST -Sex became a must and unjust
ENVY -When we betray and erotically dismay
GLUTTONY - Sucked into purgatory
WRATH - Karma will now be the beaten path
SLOTH - Killed the flame and the Moth

Seven also is the number it took for God to prove rebirth
Seven is also the number that Angels proclaim on this Earth

If you are reading this, you made it another day, the seven sins didn't win, take back your life today!
12-7-22 JJJEWELL 🖤

Let me ask you ??

So let me ask you?

When life puts you to the test, I see emotion so heavenly weighed across your chest

Questioning constantly, is my aura all too bright?
Questioning constantly, will I ever do anything right!

So let me ask you?

Does the wind feel differently when it's gently touching your face? Hope, faith, and love is here to replace

Question and constantly, when is it my time?
Questioning constantly, will it ever be mine?

So let me ask you?

Are you tired of being knocked down, it takes more muscle to frown

Quit making excuses why shit isn't going right, pick up your panties and give it one last good fight.

11-20-22 JJJEWELL 🖤

9 789357 212281